Awakening the Dark Feminine Energy

Embrace Your Inner Femme Fatale – From Self-Discovery to Confidence Mastery: The Definitive Manual for Navigating Dark Feminine Energies with Power and Poise

Shirley Stuart

Copyright © 2024. Shirley Stuart

All rights reserved. No part of this publication may be reproduced, distributed, or transmitted in any form or by any means, including photocopying, recording, or other electronic or mechanical methods, without the prior written permission of the publisher, except in the case of brief quotations embodied in critical reviews and certain other noncommercial uses permitted by copyright law.

Please Leave a Review

Dear Reader,

Thank you for choosing to read **Awakening the Dark Feminine Energy**. I hope you enjoyed the journey into the world of Dark Feminine Energy. As an independent author, your support means the world to me.

If you find **Awakening the Dark Feminine Energy** enjoyable, inspiring, or thought-provoking, I would greatly appreciate it if you could take a moment to share your thoughts by leaving a review.

Your reviews not only provide valuable feedback but also help other readers discover **Awakening the Dark Feminine Energy**. Whether it's a few sentences or a more detailed review, your words can make a significant impact.

Thank you again for your time and support. Happy reading!

Warm regards,

Shirley Stuart

BONUSES

Two powerful BONUSES are attached to this book.

THE FIRST BONUS

1. **The 90-Day Dark Feminine Energy Activation Prompt to help you practice what you'll learn in this book.**

But, how can you maximize the benefits and results of using this 90-Day Dark Feminine Activation Prompt?

It is one thing to know what to practice, but it's another thing to do it the right way.

This is why I have also attached the **SECOND BONUS**;

2. **Activation Prompt Guide**

This will explain the right mindset you'll need to have to practice effectively. It also explains the 30/90 rule and why I made it a 90-Day Dark Feminine Energy Activation Prompts

Note: You'll find these BONUSES on the pages 122 & 123 of this book.

I hope you love them, Good luck.

Table of Content

Introduction

Sisters, do you feel that fire burning inside you? The untamed passion aching to break free? I know it's there - I feel it, too. This book is a sanctuary for our inner dark goddesses craving liberation after eons of being silenced and suppressed.

I first discovered this as a teenager when my fiery spirit and sensuality were suddenly deemed liabilities. "Boys won't like you if you're too opinionated," teachers warned. "You're too much," friends whispered. My light diminished.

It wasn't until my thirties, after an abusive relationship nearly broke me, that I began the journey of excavating my lost parts and integrating my full self. Through the secret I shared in this book, long-locked doors flung open, I found freedom.

Now, I want to share the tools that helped me reclaim my worth and step fully into my power. This book guides you to unleash your dark goddess through shadow work, pleasure rituals, and sacred daily practices. You'll excavate shame, embrace defiance, and unleash your voice. Your hidden gifts will emerge.

The path is laid out in three parts:

- First, we'll dive deep into shadow work to uncover repressed emotions and learn wholeness...
- Next, we'll awaken sensual power through dance, pleasure rituals, and moontime practices...
- Finally, we'll infuse daily life with sacred feminine energy to step fully into purpose.

This journey takes courage, but you won't walk alone. Together, we'll integrate our complexity and set our untamed spirits free. We'll rise - not polished and perfect, but alive and unleashed in our power.

The call is within you. Are you ready to answer?

1

Exploring the Dark Feminine Essence

Girl, have you ever felt like there's this whole other side of yourself that you keep hidden? A bold, fierce part that doesn't always follow the "rules" and wants to roar? That's your dark feminine energy talking.

In this chapter, we're going to dive deep into that shadow side and learn why it's so freaking awesome. Society tries to tell us that dark equals bad. But we know that's BS. Our dark feminine essence is all about trusting our intuition, shedding limitations, and embracing our full power as women.

To start getting in touch with your dark goddess, let's take a field trip back in time. There are so many badass historic women who tapped into the dark feminine and shook up the status quo. Take Cleopatra - she used her sensuality, charm, and intellect to become one of the most influential rulers ever. Or Joan of Arc, who fearlessly led men into battle at just 17. Her inner warrior was lit!

These women let their dark goddess out, and so can you. What part of yourself have you been hiding because it doesn't "fit in"? The next time you feel that rebel yell bubbling up, embrace it!

Let's Time-Travel Together

Girl, let's take a little time travel adventure back to meet some of the badass historic women who embraced their dark feminine side. We can learn so much from these queens about unleashing our inner power.

First stop: Ancient Egypt. This is where we'll meet the ultimate femme fatale, Cleopatra. Cleo knew how to use her beauty, intellect, and charm to wrap the most powerful men around her finger. She was super smart and educated, speaking nine languages! Cleo used her wits and allure to navigate crazy politics and become the last pharaoh of Egypt.

Here's the thing - she owned and celebrated her sexuality and sensuality. Cleo reminds us to stop being ashamed of our desires. Tap into them! Use your dark feminine magnetism to captivate people. Cleo also showed fierce independence - she took lovers but never let them dominate her. She relied on her feminine wisdom to rule Egypt her way. Cleo is a divine inspiration to embrace our mystique and trust our inner voice.

Next up is medieval France and the legendary Joan of Arc. This brave teen believed so strongly in her divine visions that she disguised herself as a man to lead armies into battle. It took huge guts and conviction to defy gender roles like that in the 1500s! Joan was also super devout in her faith - she faced intense criticism from religious leaders who called her a heretic. But she stood firm in what she believed was right.

Joan shows us what it means to fiercely stand up for what we believe in, no matter what anyone else thinks. She guides us to embrace our rebellious side, protect our vision, and stay true to our values. Joan followed her inner divine light to do what was right, not what was easy. When we feel doubt creep in, Joan inspires us to dig deep for courage and act boldly.

Finally, we'll time travel to the roaring 1920s to chill with Clara Bow - Hollywood's first "It Girl." As one of the film's earliest sex symbols, Clara broke all the rules with her bold sexuality and wild child antics. She totally owned her sex appeal in an era when that was scandalous for actresses. Clara partied hard with the hottest stars of the day. She lived life completely on her terms.

Clara teaches us the power of letting our freak flag fly and defining ourselves, not letting society do it for us. She inspires us to let loose, live out loud, enjoy life and our bodies. Clara refused to be tamed or conform. She had a rough childhood but didn't let it break her. Clara shows that our dark feminine side is about resilience, freedom of expression, and a touch of delightful rebellion.

The struggles we deal with today - feeling invisible, misunderstood, pressured to conform - are SO not new. Women have faced that for centuries. But badass women like Cleopatra, Joan of Arc, and Clara Bow unlocked their inner dark goddess. They blazed a trail for us to do the same.

Let the stories of these queens inspire you on your journey. You've got this, soul sister. Their dark feminine magic courses through you, too. Time to claim your place in the cosmic sisterhood of empowered women!

Feeling It Out

So why does society make us feel bad about our dark side? Well, strong, independent women are hard to control. We threaten rigid roles and norms when we stop dimming our light. But trying to conform only hurts us. The patriarchy wants to tame us by instilling shame and doubt.

But it's alright; now that we've connected with our historical queens, it's time to start embracing your dark traits. I've got some cool exercises to help you tap into that inner dark goddess. Grab your journal and get ready to explore.

Let's start with a shadow exploration. Set a timer for 5 minutes. Close your eyes. Take some deep breaths.

Think back to times when you felt fiery, rebellious, or different. Don't judge, observe. What did those moments look or feel like? What part of yourself were you hiding?

Write down any shadow traits or feelings that surfaced. For me, it's my intimate side that craves touch and closeness. I muted it to avoid shame. I also unearthed my stubbornness and refusal to ask for help when I struggle.

Remember, our shadows are simply parts of ourselves that we've kept hidden. Embrace them with love. They have unique gifts, not just flaws.

Another exercise is to create an alter ego. On paper, dream up a bold, empowered persona. Give the alter ego a name, style, and attitude. What does she represent about you? Now, write a journal entry from her perspective. How does she view your life, dreams, and challenges? Let this foil character give you insight into your inner badass.

Venting through writing can also unveil your dark side. Set a timer for 10 minutes. Write furiously about situations that make you angry or resentful. Curse, rant, dig deep! Don't hold back. Get it all out on paper. Look for recurring themes in what you write. These moments often reveal suppressed aspects of ourselves.

I also recommend dancing wildly to music with a heavy, sensual beat. Move those hips, run your hands along your body, close your eyes, and improvise as the music guides you. Feeling the rhythm in our bones awakens the dark feminine.

To say piss off to the patriarchy, we must radically accept every part of our dark selves with love. These practices help us reclaim those lost pieces and step into our power. Free your inner dark goddess, my Queen! She's waiting for you.

Defining Your Dark Side

Alright, ladies, it's time for some creative vision boarding to define exactly what your dark feminine side looks like. This is about making your own rules - no box-checking allowed!

Gather some magazines, printouts of affirmations, fabric, glitter, whatever speaks to you. Now, start a vision board that captures your unique dark goddess essence. Are you drawn to bold colors or gothic blacks? Nature images or powerful women? Luxury items or activist quotes? Follow your intuition.

I'm seeing ripped-out pics of Stevie Nicks, Frida Kahlo, and forests. Affirmations like "I am untamed" and "My power awakens." Gold glitter and crimson fabric swatches. What's taking shape for you?

Get detailed with visuals about your shadow qualities, too. Find images that symbolize your sneakiness, lust, defiance, cunning, wrath, mischief - whatever you've unearthed within. Paste them with pride! These traits are part of your magic.

My board has a ruby ring for passion, cat eyes for mystery, snakes for sneakiness, and flames for bottled-up anger. I'm acknowledging and honoring those parts of myself.

Now for the finishing touches. What overall message do you want your vision board to project? Arrange and add elements around that intention. Need a boost of courage? Surround it with fierce warrior women. Want to call in love? Dot your board with hearts and roses.

I added lotus flowers to inspire growth through adversity. Goddess depictions to embrace divine feminine wisdom. And the phrase "I flourish freely" is my reminder to live boldly in my power. My dark side defined my way.

What does your dark feminine essence include? Define this on your terms, soul sis. When you fully claim these qualities and stop hiding, that's when your inner Queen emerges. She can't wait to see the true you in all your shades of light and dark. Let her shine through!

2

Embracing the Shadows

Sisters, it's time to stop dimming our light! Society wants to put us ladies in a neat little box with strict rules on how to act - be pleasant, be decent, and be "ladylike." But we aren't manicured poodles here to perform. We are glorious wolves howling at the moon!

Inside each of us are unique shadows - sneakiness, sexuality, defiance, ambition, wrath. The traits that patriarchal norms demand we hide or deny. But repressing them only shrinks our lives and numbs our joy. We cannot split ourselves in two, denying whole aspects to fit in.

When we lock away those shadow parts, it's like caging a wild animal. Eventually, it will break free unless it withers and dies first. Wolf or poodle, you choose. But wolf packs are way more fun!

Sisters, it's time to break from our cages! No more muzzles, no more shame. We must learn to embrace our shadows as vital parts of ourselves. The key is expressing, not repressing. Bring your shadows into the light and watch your spirit thrive.

I'm talking late-night dancing to pulsing beats, writing furious, uncensored words, and singing with drunken abandon. However, it bubbles up; let your shadows speak. Be the wolf howling from mountain peaks, terrifying those who wish you tame.

Our shadows hold immense power - cunning, sexuality, rebellion, passion. As women reclaim this, the patriarchy trembles. Rise and roar! Fearlessly embrace your whole self, shadows and all. Blind them with your glorious light.

Who among us will be the first to break free? Who will be the first to say NO to conformity and soul-sucking obedience? Beauty lies not in denying the dark, but helming its power unashamed. I see your soul's glow behind anxious eyes. Together, we will tear off our muzzles and flood the world with our light!

Shadow Self 101

It's time to get personal and unveil the unique traits of our shadow selves. Grab your journal; we're going inner spelunking!

To warm up, write for 10 minutes nonstop about your childhood and teen years. When did you feel different, weird, or like you had to hide? Don't censor; get it all down.

For me, I was teased for my hairy arms and bushy brows. I learned to obsess over shaving and plucking. I also had a temper and got labeled "combustible." I funneled my fire into achiever mode and people-pleasing, thinking those traits were bad.

Now, review what you wrote. Highlight any behaviors, feelings, or qualities that you muted or felt shame about. Pick the top three traits you learned to hide.

I unearthed my body hair: defiance, ambition, and fiery anger. Those all got stuffed down by society's norms. But no more!

Time to make friends with your shadow side. For each trait, write an understanding. Like "My body hair is natural, just like my passions." Or "My ambition drives me to make an impact." Reframe them as gifts!

Also, try embodying those shadows through dance. Crank the music and move in ways that channel those repressed parts of you. Shake loose the shame!

Finally, meditate on accepting your full self, shadows included. Picture you as a child when those parts first emerged. Send her unconditional love. We were all born wild until the world told us to be tame.

Integrating our shadows is about reclaiming exiled aspects of our spirit. What unique blend makes up your soul? You are so much more than society's narrow image. Embrace your full power!

Own it, Babe

It's time to stop hiding the parts of yourself that society deems "dark" or "bad." Your jealousy, anger, sadness, sexuality, ambition – these alleged flaws are what make you beautifully complex. So own them, Babe. Make these shadows your superpowers.

Start by writing yourself some badass daily affirmations that celebrate your dark side. Maybe something like: "My jealousy shows how much I care." Or: "My ambition makes me unstoppable." Find mantras that make your darkness your BFF.

Then, visualize yourself as a woman who's got all her shades on. Picture yourself standing tall in an outfit that highlights your dark side. Maybe you're wearing a bold red lip, a leather jacket, and thigh-high boots. See your confident strut and hear your uncompromising voice. This is you with your darkness on full display. Own it.

The world wants women to be one-dimensional – to fit neatly in a box labeled "sweet" or "pleasant." So let's get messy. Embrace the witch, the villainess, the anti-heroine within. Your complexity is your strength. You contain multitudes – light and dark. Love and own every piece of your intricate soul. You deserve to live as your fullest, most authentic self. The shadows are part of you, Babe. So wear them proudly today.

Rolling with the Punches

Discovering your dark side can bring up some weird feelings. One minute you're pumped to embrace your inner anti-heroine; the next, you're freaking out. "Am I going too far?" "What will people think?" It's totally normal to feel some fear and hesitation as your shadow self comes into the light. This stuff can be intense! Here are some tips to roll with the punches:

- Go at your own pace. Don't force yourself to share or reveal more than you're ready for. Baby steps are cool.

- Vent to someone you trust. Talking it out can help relieve the stress. Choose a friend who won't judge.

- Channel the feels into art. Paint, write, sing, or dance out those emotions. Get creative and expressive.

- Try a mantra. Repeat phrases like "I accept myself, darkness and all."

- Take a timeout when it gets overwhelming. Do some yoga, meditate, or go for a walk to clear your head.

Owning your shadow side changes your whole vibe. You stand a little taller and speak a little bolder. You're no longer hiding pieces of yourself, so you radiate authenticity. People may react in different ways. Some may seem uncomfortable with the "new" you. Let them adjust at their own pace. Others will appreciate and relate to your realness. The coolest ones? They'll reveal their hidden depths.

Keep going on this journey. With time, it gets easier to roll with the punches. Soon, you'll wear your shadows as comfortably as your fave leather jacket. Until then, be patient with yourself. You got this.

3

Self-Love and Acceptance

Girl, I see you rolling your eyes already at the words "self-love." Bear with me for a second. I know the whole self-love movement is a major cringe sometimes. All those influencers posing with green juice talking about ~self-care~. We get it.

But all the woo-woo doesn't mean self-love isn't vital. Because, at its core, it's about acceptance. And sis, you deserve to accept yourself. Shadows and all.

I know it's easier said than done. We all have those critical voices in our heads telling us we don't measure up. Our flaws shout the loudest. The world is quick to point out what's "wrong" with us, too. It's hard not to get down on yourself.

Here's the truth, though: you're a boss, Babe, work in progress. We all are. You're already doing amazing just by taking this journey to embrace your dark side. Give yourself props for that!

The more you learn to accept every piece of yourself, the more you can see your unique beauty. Self-love isn't about thinking you're perfect. It's about loving yourself through the highs and lows.

So yeah, self-love is for you, too, Queen. No filter or green juice is required. Let's talk about how to start accepting all of your magnificent, messy self in this chapter. The self-love revolution starts here.

Queen of Your Heart - Love Letters to You

One of the best ways to practice self-love is to write love letters to yourself literally. I know it can feel corny at first, but stick with me. Sit down with a pen and paper and get ready to gush about your favorite person – you!

Address the love letter to yourself. Then, let the compliments flow. Brag about your talents, skills, accomplishments, and inner beauty. Don't hold back – you're writing to the woman you admire most. Tell yourself all the things you wish others said about you. Describe how amazing, capable, sexy, funny, and strong you are. Write from a place of complete adoration for yourself.

When you're finished, keep these love letters somewhere special. Re-read them when you need a confidence boost. The more you affirm your worth, the more you start to believe it. Consider writing yourself a new love letter weekly, or anytime you're feeling down. The pen-to-paper act makes it more powerful. Watch as this practice fills your heart with love for your badass self!

Bullet Journal Your Love Story with Yourself

Grab your bullet journal or notebook. You're going to create pages dedicated to your journey of self-love. Here are some ideas:

- Make a playlist of songs that make you feel like a queen. Add lyrics and doodles.
- List 50 things you love about yourself. Decoratively write them out.
- Track empowering daily habits like meditation, journaling, and exercise.
- Paste inspiring quotes, magazine cutouts, and pics of fierce women who represent you.
- Record breakthrough moments when you chose self-love over self-criticism.
- Write encouraging notes to yourself when you need a boost.

Your bullet journal will chronicle the ongoing love story between you and your badass self! Let it guide you in nurturing your spirit every day.

Look Yourself in the Mirror and Say, "Damn, I'm Amazing!"

This may feel silly, but it works. Stand in front of a mirror and give yourself some serious hype. Look into your own eyes as you declare how smart, gorgeous, strong, and phenomenal you are. Speak with sincerity, authority, and love. Don't break eye contact with yourself! Keep the compliments coming until you truly start to believe them.

The more you vocally hype yourself up, the more your self-talk will change. Shifting your inner dialogue is key to self-love and acceptance. So grab every chance you get to cheer yourself on — even if it seems awkward at first. Own the fact that you are amazing, girl. Your reflection deserves to hear it!

Forgive and Forget Yourself

Being hard on yourself will only damage your self-esteem and get in the way of self-love. Instead, learn techniques to offer yourself compassion when you've messed up or feel inadequate. Forgiving yourself takes practice but gets easier over time. Soon, you'll be able to brush off mistakes and keep your head held high.

Write a Forgiveness Letter to Yourself

When you're disappointed in something you've done, write yourself a heartfelt letter of forgiveness. Start by admitting what happened without judgment. Explore the deeper emotions that led to it. Offer yourself complete absolution – you're allowed to make mistakes! Set intentions to grow. End with encouragement and love for your imperfectly human self.

Keep this letter to refer back to whenever you need self-forgiveness. The act of writing it is healing. It's proof that you deserve kindness, not criticism. We all slip up sometimes. Learn to let it go and move forward with self-love intact.

Guided Meditation for Self-Criticism

A short meditation can re-center you in self-acceptance when your inner critic doesn't shut up. Get comfortable and close your eyes. Notice any negative self-talk without judgment. Gently set those voices aside. Silently repeat positive mantras like "I am enough" while feeling your heart open with warmth.

Use this meditation to remember you don't have to be perfect to be worthy of self-love. Being flawed is part of the human experience. Treat yourself with the same gentle understanding you would a close friend who made a mistake. You are always enough.

Practicing consistent self-forgiveness will transform your relationship with yourself. You'll grow more secure in knowing all people stumble sometimes, and that's okay. Your worth remains unchanged despite any missteps. So be gentle with yourself. Don't waste energy beating yourself up over being human. Simply learn and move forward with your head held high.

Everyday Self-Love Magic

Self-love isn't just about occasional practices like writing yourself letters or meditating. Make it a daily lifestyle by weaving little acts of self-care and affirmation into your routine habits. Soon, nurturing yourself will become second nature.

Affirmation Challenge – Let's Make Self-Love Trendy

Affirmations work by literally reprogramming your self-talk. So, commit to repeating positive mantras daily. Write or recite affirmations that celebrate your strengths, talents, beauty, and worth. Say them while looking in the mirror, in the car, before bed – anytime!

Here are some examples:

- I am powerful.

- I love every piece of me.

- I am bold and unstoppable.

- I nurture my mind, body, and spirit.

Make your affirmations specific and unique to you. Craft mantras that target your needs, dreams, and areas for growth. Repeat them genuinely with love and authority. Make this a consistent practice, and watch your self-love grow.

Apologize to Yourself for Past Self-Criticism – Because You Deserve Better

We've all spent years beating ourselves up unnecessarily about our looks, choices, abilities, etc. It's time to right those wrongs. Take a moment to officially apologize to yourself for the excessive self-criticism of your past. You deserved compassion back then, not judgment.

Write a letter or speak out loud. Ask your younger self for forgiveness. Tell her all the ways she was actually amazing, even if she couldn't see it. Vow to stop the negative self-talk moving forward. You're going to treat yourself with the patience, respect, and care you deserve from now on. We all make mistakes, but you won't shame yourself for them anymore. You're going to be your own #1 fan.

Small, consistent acts of self-love magic will transform how you relate to yourself. Make self-care not just a one-time practice but an everyday lifestyle. You deserve to feel valued, appreciated, and respected by the most important person in your world – you! So weave little rituals of self-love into all you do.

4

Mastering Body Language

Girl, have you ever noticed how much you can tell about someone just from their body language? The way they walk, stand, gesture, make eye contact (or don't)? Our bodies have a whole language of their own that reveals how we really feel underneath the surface.

And here's the tea — we have more power than we realize to influence others through our physical presence. With the right body language, you can command respect, establish authority, and broadcast your confidence to the world.

But, of course, it's not always that simple. Insecurities, doubts, and bad habits can creep into our body language and undermine the vibe we want to give off. That's why consciously mastering how you physically show up is so crucial.

In this chapter, we'll break down specific techniques for body language that assert your bold, badass energy. You'll learn gestures that display confidence, stance modifications that project strength, eye contact hacks that establish dominance in a room, and much more.

Imagine walking into any space and instantly commanding people's attention and admiration through your phenomenal physical presence alone. Intriguing, right? Your body has genius potential...let's unlock it!

Turn on your Magnetic Vibes

The way you physically carry yourself sends nonverbal cues that can either attract people or push them away.

Let's master body language that energetically draws others in and makes you utterly magnetic.

Body Language 101

Before modifying your physical presence, it helps to understand the psychology behind different mannerisms. For example, crossed arms signal defensiveness. Fidgeting hands betray anxiety. A slouched posture conveys low confidence.

Make a real effort to notice body language all around you – from strangers, friends, family, and yourself. What does it reveal? Train your eye to decipher the secret stories our physicality tells.

Understand the Secret Language Your Body's Been Speaking All Along

Once you get better at "reading" body language, turn the analysis on yourself. What vibe have you been transmitting through your posture, gestures, and eye contact? Do these habits serve your goals? Or have you unconsciously been projecting insecurity and disconnect?

Pay attention to your mannerisms during interactions. Are you standing tall or slumping? Making eye contact or looking away? Leaning in or distancing yourself? Your body speaks volumes without you even realizing it. Become fluent in its language.

Strut Your Stuff – Practice Confident Body Language with Swagger

Now that you're more aware of your physical habits, it's time to upgrade your body language! Practice moves that convey boldness and confidence:

- Take up space – spread out! Sit or stand with wide elbows and open knees. Claim your area.

- Stand and walk tall – keep your chin up and shoulders back. Imagine a string pulling you straight.

- Limit fidgeting – keep hands still at your sides or clasped behind your back. Exude calm.

- Make direct eye contact – lock eyes with confidence. Don't be the first to break contact!

- Slow down movements – act deliberately rather than rushing. You have authority.

- Minimize crossed arms – keep them open.

The more you physically embody assurance and power, the more natural it will feel. Fake it till you make it, Queen! Body language is a skill that develops with practice. Soon, you'll be attracting tons of positive attention without saying a word.

Feminine Vibes Only

Owning a space with your body language doesn't have to feel masculine. Let's explore moves that assert power and confidence through an unapologetically feminine lens.

Journal Your Moments of Boss Body Language

Pay attention as you go about your days for times when you naturally display bold physical presence. Maybe you commanded a room at a party or aced a job interview through your body language alone.

Jot down what worked in a journal. How did you carry yourself? What were your gestures, posture, walking, eye contact, etc.? Capture your moments of shining feminine power through physicality.

Review your journal to identify your signature moves. Then, intentionally replicate them to tap into that energy again. Note how people react when you embody dominant feminine energy through body language.

Use Body Language In Everyday Situations – Let's Make Every Room Yours

Practice elevating your physical presence during the following:

Meetings: Sit at the heads of tables. Stand tall. Limit fidgeting. Make eye contact when speaking.

Parties: Enter with chin up, shoulders back. Slowly survey the room. Hug friends loosely rather than clinging.

Dates: Lean back to claim your space. Limit crossed legs. Gesture with palms up.

Interviews: Walk in smoothly with head high. Shake hands firmly. Keep limbs open.

With consistent effort, you'll carry yourself powerfully without thinking. Chin up, chest out, eyes forward. Feel that natural confidence flow through your body language. You were born to take up space unapologetically! Use your physicality to command every room.

Charisma Explosion

Charisma is that mysterious "it factor" that instantly draws people to you. But the truth is, charisma can absolutely be developed and amplified. Let's find your magnetism and allow it to explode into the room.

Be Your Charisma Idol – Copy Those Confident Queens Around You

Pay close attention to the women you find utterly magnetic. It may be a public figure, boss at work, teacher, or friend. What makes their energy so charismatic?

Take notes on their body language, speech patterns, style, and presence. Do they speak slowly and make eye contact? Use expressive hand gestures? Wear bold colors and stand tall. Identify their charisma triggers.

Now, embody those traits in your way. Experiment with speaking calmly, dressing sharply, and holding eye contact. Find what works for you and makes you feel confident in command. Model women with captivating presences to uncover your charisma.

Public Speaking Exercises to Unleash Your Inner Leader

One of the fastest ways to build charismatic energy is by practicing public speaking. Start small by simply speaking aloud at home. Build up to larger audiences.

Try recording speeches on your phone to review. Master maintaining eye contact, varied tone and open body language. Take an improv or public speaking class.

Volunteer to make presentations at school or in your community. The more you put yourself out there authentically, the more your magnetism will grow.

Owning the room comes naturally when you tap into your inner power and light. Keep observing influential women. Experiment with embodying their essence. Public speaking forces you to project charismatic energy – so do it often! Let your inner leader take center stage.

5

Emotional Reflection Prompts

Girl, this self-empowerment journey is going to stir up all the emotions. We've laughed together, raged together, cried together. And we still have a ways to go!

So, before we continue, let's take a moment to reflect on our feelings. I'll give you some writing prompts to explore your experiences so far – the good, bad, ugly, beautiful, and everything in between.

Be prepared to dive deep into your inner world through journaling. Don't hold back! This is a judgment-free zone. Be brutally honest with yourself. The more vulnerable you get on paper, the more you'll understand your growth.

Sound like therapy? It is! Just cheaper. And you get to write in your PJs while eating cookies. Plus, no awkward silences while you think of what to confess next. It's all you, Babe.

These prompts will help you process new insights about your dark side and release any negativity holding you back. You'll uncover so much wisdom within yourself, girl. Our feelings make us beautifully human.

So grab your journal, pens, candies, tissues, whatever you need. Find a quiet, comfy spot. Take a few deep breaths. And let's start reflecting!

Feel It All, Babe

Okay, sis, before we can fully unleash that inner dark goddess, we've got to address the feels. I know you've been taught to stuff down your emotions, to mute your reactions, to keep it all inside. That stops now.

Journaling Extravaganza

I want you to start journaling ALL your feelings – no editing, no filtering, just pure, unadulterated YOU spilling out onto the page. When you're pissed, write about it. When you're heartbroken, weep into your journal. This is a judgment-free zone to pour your heart out.

Some prompts to get you started:

- What are you angry about lately? Don't hold back; go on a multi-page rant if you need to.
- When was the last time your feelings were hurt? Write a letter to the person who hurt you.

- What secret dreams do you have that you've been afraid to share? Describe them in vivid detail.

Create a Journal That's As Extra As Your Emotions

While you're journaling, I want you to let your creative juices flow. Decorate those pages with glitter pens, magazine cutouts, inspirational quotes – whatever speaks to you. Make it colorful, make it messy, make it as fabulously extra as your inner world. This is your sacred space to emote, so don't hold back.

Some ideas:

- Collage pages related to different emotions – one for joy, one for anger, one for hurt.

- Doodle patterns or shapes that capture your mood.

- Tape in photos, ticket stubs, and letters from old friends – visual mementos of meaningful moments.

The key is not censoring yourself. Get it all out there, Babe. Cry onto the pages if you need to. Your journal is where your raw, uncensored emotions can flow freely. It's going to be messy and wild – but so are you. That's the beauty.

Keep digging in and expressing ALL the feels, my sister. It's time to embrace your complexity and stop bottling yourself up. Get ready for a journey of self-discovery and radical self-acceptance. This is just the beginning...

Turning Pain into Power Playlist

Music can be medicine, sister. The right songs can help transmute pain into power and get you excited when you're feeling low. Let's make you a custom playlist to turn up when you need a boost.

Identify a Tough Emotional Moment and Find the Beats That Make It Empowering

Think back to a challenging time that really tested your resilience. Maybe a bad breakup, the loss of a loved one, or a career setback. It likely brought up some heavy, difficult emotions.

Now, make a playlist of songs that pump you up and make you feel strong when you reflect on that experience. Some examples:

- "Survivor" by Destiny's Child for when you showed your strength.
- "Fighter" by Christina Aguilera to embrace your fighter spirit.
- "Rise Up" by Andra Day when you want to lift yourself.

Aim for 5-10 songs that make you feel motivated, resilient, and powerful when you think of rising above that painful time. Blast it when you need a confidence boost!

Daily Emotional Check-In – Let's Get Those Feels in Check

Moving forward, take 5 minutes each morning to check in on your emotional state and create mini playlists for what you need that day.

Are you feeling stressed? Make a "Power Down" playlist with soothing, zen tunes to relax. Feeling sad? Create a "Lift Me Up" mix of upbeat inspirational anthems. Angry? Curate some ragers to help you process the rage. The goal is to become more aware of your emotions day-to-day and give them a musical voice.

Get ready to unleash your feelings, Babe! Music is medicine, so let's use it to amplify and honor whatever you're going through. You got this!

6

Actionable Steps for Empowerment

Alright, girl, we've done the inner work – now it's time to take action and make some actual moves towards your goals. I know you've got huge dreams simmering under the surface. Maybe you want to start your own business. Maybe you want to leave a toxic relationship. Maybe you're ready to apply for that dream job finally.

Whatever your ambitious goals, this chapter provides concrete steps to start making them happen. No more just fantasizing about the future – we're getting strategic and mapping out plans to manifest your dreams, one step at a time.

I'll walk you through how to break down big goals into bite-sized milestones, so you don't get overwhelmed. We'll work on overcoming limiting beliefs, building up your confidence, and shutting down your inner critic.

You'll learn how to:

-        Identify roadblocks and reframe them as opportunities. If something feels hard or scary, embrace it as a chance to grow!

-        Build a supportive community of badass women who will cheer you on as you go after your goals. Accountability is key!

-        Celebrate small wins along the way. Every milestone achieved deserves a victory dance – keep that momentum going!

Basically, we're going to plan out how to push outside your comfort zone and systematically make your dreams a reality. It's time to stop waiting for "someday" – the work starts now, Babe!

I'll be right by your side, providing encouragement, guidance, and actionable steps tailored to YOU. Let's do this – and never forget to celebrate yourself every step of the way. You deserve it!

Goal-Getter Queen

Dream big, Babe! Let's get clear on your goals and start taking steps to achieve them. No more hiding your ambitions – it's time to boldly go after what you want.

Vision Board Upgrade

Grab some magazines, print out inspirational quotes, and find images that represent your biggest goals and dreams. Get creative and make a vision board to keep you focused and motivated. Leave space to add to it as you accomplish milestones!

Make your vision board really speak to YOU. Get specific – want to start a nonprofit? Find logos of ones you admire. Dream job? Print out job listings and company profiles. Dream partner? Make a list of must-have qualities. Infuse it with affirmations like "I am a boss bitch capable of achieving anything I set my mind to."

Put your vision board somewhere you'll see it daily. Let it be a visual reminder of how abundant life can be if you dare to dream big and work for what you want.

Break Down Big Goals Into Steps – Let's Conquer Them Together

Look at your biggest, most ambitious goal. Now, break it down into smaller mini-goals that are totally doable. If your big goal is to start a business, your steps may be:

- Research business models and decide on a niche

- Take online courses on entrepreneurship

- Create a business plan and budget

- Contact suppliers or vendors

- Design branding and marketing materials

- Set up a business bank account and financing

- File all legal paperwork to establish business

- Launch pilot program or start operations

See how it becomes less intimidating? Just tackle one step at a time. I'll be here to help brainstorm action plans and provide support when you feel overwhelmed. You got this, Queen!

Keep chipping away with discipline. Even small progress will start to compound and build your confidence. You have so much untapped potential – let's unleash it together. Now dazzle the world with your goals, you ambitious goddess!

Manifesto for a Queen

It's time to get fired up about your goals, lady! Let's write a bold manifesto to rally your inner badass.

Write a Manifesto That's As Fierce As You Are

Grab a journal or blank wall space. Now, write a statement of purpose all about your biggest goals, dreams, and the powerful woman you are becoming.

Some tips:

- Get specific on what you want to achieve
- Speak in positive affirmations ("I am a force of nature," "I am unstoppable")
- Infuse it with attitude ("I will own every damn room I walk into," "I bow down to no one")
- Let your inner rebel out ("I honor no rules but my own," "I blaze my trail")

Your manifesto should ignite that inner flame and spark ambition. Re-read it when you need motivation. This is the new fierce you – now go out and conquer!

Celebrate Every Tiny Success – You're On Fire!

On your path to big goals, be sure to celebrate the small wins along the way. Did you send a cold email to an influencer you admire? Throw yourself a mini-dance party! Finally hit submit on that college application. Treat yourself to a latte!

Celebrating small milestones builds momentum and keeps motivation high. Take a moment to soak in that feeling of accomplishment, no matter how minor it may seem. You're doing the work – now give that badass woman in the mirror a pat on the back!

I'll be here with pom poms, confetti, and an air horn, cheering you on every step of the way. Get them, Queen – you shine bright like a diamond!

Party Time!

Accomplishing goals deserves a proper celebration, my Queen! Let's get you amped up to crush it.

Establish a Reward System for Slaying Those Goals

Decide on rewards you'll give yourself when you meet targets along your journey. Make them fun treats that will keep you motivated! Some ideas:

- Spa day after nailing that big presentation
- Shopping spree for getting into your top college
- Dinner party when you land the promotion
- Weekend getaway after hitting startup fundraising goal

Build anticipation for each milestone reward. Focus on enjoying the journey and the process, not just the destination. You deserve to feel proud of every step forward!

Reflect on Your Growth – Adjust Goals Like the Boss You Are

Every few months, take time to reflect on your progress and learnings. Review your original goals – what worked? What didn't? Any new priorities or dreams you want to tackle next?

Don't be afraid to edit your goals and change course. Growth means evolving. Document lessons learned to help plan your next chapter.

Celebrate how far you've come, then look ahead to the horizon. Dream big for what's next, adjust your goals, and keep boldly moving forward. You got this, superstar!

Remember, it's not just about achievements – it's about discovering who you want to become. I'm so proud of how you're spreading your wings and soaring! Now go out there and keep dazzling the world, you goal-crushing goddess!

7

Navigating Relationships with Power

Alright, girl, it's time for some real talk about relationships. I know you've spent too much time dimming your light for unworthy partners. You've suppressed your needs to keep the peace and given your power away. No more!

This chapter is all about learning to navigate relationships, romantic and otherwise, in a way that honors your worth. I'll teach you how to:

- Communicate your needs and set boundaries without apology. Your desires matter.

- Spot red flags early so you don't waste time on the wrong people. Trust your intuition!

- Exude a powerful, queenly energy that commands respect. Channel your inner goddess.

- Walk away from any relationship that makes you feel small. You deserve better.

It's time to stop minimizing yourself in relationships and start taking up space. I'll share techniques to have tough talks while keeping your cool so you can vocalize your perspective fearlessly.

You'll gain tools to foster healthy connections that amplify your voice, not silence it. Strategies to firmly call out disrespect. Mindsets to radiate a vibe that says, "I'm a prize; treat me as such."

Of course, there will be messy moments and growing pains, too. I'll be right here to walk you through them.

Together, we'll transform how you operate in relationships so you always feel valued and empowered.

Get ready to level up and start relating like the Queen you are! Your connections are about to get a whole lot deeper and more fulfilling. Let's do this.

Queen of Relationships

It's time to get clear on your standards, Babe. Crafting a self-respect checklist will help you identify dealbreakers and know when to walk away.

Self-Respect Checklist

Make a list of your absolute must-haves in relationships, as well as behaviors you won't tolerate. Get specific – ex. "My partner must make me feel safe and supported," or "I refuse to be with someone who lies or cheats."

Some areas to define:

- Shared values

- Communication style

- Anger management

- Emotional maturity

- Intimacy needs

Post your checklist somewhere visible. Use it to evaluate new connections and flag any red flags early. Most importantly, follow through – if a relationship stops aligning with your standards, you're out. Don't compromise on these!

Journal About a Time You Set Boundaries and Felt Amazing

Write about an instance where you stood firm on a boundary or walked away when your needs weren't being met. How did enforcing your standards make you feel? What did you learn?

Remember this empowering experience whenever you need the courage to stand your ground. You deserve partners who meet your needs without reluctance. Nicely request changes, but be ready to move on if they can't get on board.

You are a queen – never forget that. Now, go forth and forge connections that make you feel valued, respected, and utterly fabulous. The right people will celebrate your standards, not resist them.

Assertiveness Training

Time to find your voice, Babe! Let's practice speaking up for yourself while remaining cool, calm, and collected.

Practice Assertive Communication – It's Not Rude; It's Royal

Being assertive means expressing your needs and perspective without being aggressive. Some tips:

- Use "I" statements ("I feel concerned when plans get changed last minute.")

- Be direct but not accusatory ("I need you to call if you'll be late so I can plan my evening.")

- Focus on resolving the issue, not attacking the person

- Remain poised – no yelling or drama

- Stand firm if met with resistance

Role-play scenarios with friends to build confidence. The more you assert yourself, the more natural it will feel. This is the communication style of a queen – direct, self-assured, and unapologetic.

Real-Life Examples of Women Who Turned Assertiveness Into Empowerment

Read up on trailblazing women who used their voice to drive change – Rosa Parks, Malala Yousafzai, Ruth Bader

Ginsburg. What can you learn from how they spoke truth to power?

Whenever you need motivation, look to their example. Channel their courage as you stand up for your worth. Your experiences and perspective matter – don't let anyone silence you.

With grace and tenacity, keep speaking your mind and asserting your needs. You are worthy of being heard. And remember – real power lies in using your voice. You got this, Queen!

Queen's Guide to Healthy Relationships

Know your worth and accept nothing less, my Queen. Let's break down what emotionally healthy relationships look like.

Characteristics of a Healthy Relationship – Don't Settle for Less

- Mutual trust, respect and honesty
- Open communication and vulnerability
- Supporting each other's growth and goals
- Compromise when conflict arises
- Feelings of safety and comfort to be yourself
- chemistry and passion

Do an audit of your relationships – are these present? Don't make excuses for those who don't meet your standards.

Actionable Steps: How to Communicate Effectively in Your Relationships

Here are some effective ways to communicate in your relationships;

- Listen actively without interrupting

- Validate the other person's perspective before asserting your own
- Use "I" statements to take ownership of your view
- If things get heated, take a break and revisit when calm
- Compromise when possible, stand firm when necessary
- Check-in on the relationship health regularly

Bring your full, authentic self to your connections. Never shy away from the tough talks – communication is the foundation. You deserve to feel empowered in all your relationships, so keep speaking up until you do!

8

Embracing Sexuality and Sensuality

Alright, sis, let's dive into a spicy but important topic – getting in touch with your sensual, sexual self. I know society has filled your head with shame around owning your desires. But your sexuality is a gift, not something to repress.

In this chapter, we'll undo all that harmful conditioning and explore your intimacy needs honestly and without judgment. I'll share tantric practices to awaken your senses and get in touch with your erotic energy. You'll learn techniques to boost confidence in the bedroom while still respecting your boundaries.

We'll cover:

- Communicating fantasies and desires boldly and shame-free

- Learning your body's pleasure points through sensual self-touch

- Setting sexual standards and vetting partners

- Establishing intimacy that's emotionally safe and satisfying

Consider this permission to embrace your sensuality in all its messy, flawed glory. To honor your cravings without apology or inhibition. Your passion is divine - it's time to let it ignite.

Get ready to kindle the flames of desire on YOUR terms. No more repressing your primal nature. Your pleasure and fulfillment matter – so let's start prioritizing both. Say goodbye to shame and start celebrating your sexuality openly and proudly!

Celebrating Your Sensuality

Let's keep expanding how you relate to your sensuality and sexuality, goddess.

Tantric Practices

Explore tantric breathing, movement, and massage. These practices harness sexual energy for full mind/body awareness.

Try sensual dancing to music, self-massage with oils, and eye gazing with a partner. Go slow, relax into the present moment, and awaken your senses.

Define Your Comfort Zone

What feels comfortable for you sensually, and what doesn't yet? Outline clear boundaries so you can healthily expand your horizon.

Maybe you enjoy kissing and massage but aren't ready for oral sex. Or you love using toys solo but aren't comfortable introducing them to a partner. Defining your edge will help you grow at your own pace.

Surround Yourself with Sex-Positivity

Follow creators providing healthy perspectives on sex. Immerse yourself in messages that celebrate sexuality as natural.

Check out intimacy coaches, ethical porn, feminist erotica, and sex toy companies promoting empowerment. Shift your mindset by exposing yourself to sex-positive resources.

Keep learning and shedding stigma, queen. Your desires are a beautiful part of you – get ready to embrace them fully!

Empowerment in the Bedroom

Ladies, the bedroom is one space where we often dim our power, afraid to speak our true desires. But pleasure is our birthright! Tapping into our dark feminine energy means owning our sensuality and confidently communicating what we crave without hesitation. Let's unleash our intimate confidence.

Actionable Steps: How to Communicate Your Desires Confidently

Here are actionable steps you can take to communicate your desires confidently;

- Know your boundaries and needs. If unfamiliar with a partner, discuss them before getting intimate.

- Give feedback on what feels good and what you want more/less of. Don't just let things happen to you – help co-create the experience.

- Compliment your partner when they do something you enjoy. Positive reinforcement builds intimacy.

- If something doesn't feel right, speak up or stop the encounter. You are in charge of your comfort.

Guest Stories: Women Who Transformed Their Sexual Experiences Through Empowerment

Finding community fuels bedroom empowerment, too. "I finally told my boyfriend how I like to be touched. It was awkward but so worth it! Now our sex life is transformed," shares Aisha, 21.

Owning our sensuality moves us past shame about our bodies and pleasure. As women reclaim this dark feminine power, intimacy transforms from repressive to ecstatic. Nothing is hotter than a woman who boldly speaks her desires!

Keep expanding your mindset and skills, my Queen. You deserve an intimate life as rich, fulfilling, and radiant as you are.

Safe Sex, Empowered Sex

When we take charge of our sexual health, we can feel fully empowered in our intimate experiences.

Let's make sure we're being smart while getting intimate, Queen.

Practical Tips for Safe Sex and Empowered Choices

- Set boundaries and stick to them. Don't do anything you aren't comfortable with. Prioritize your needs.

- Always use protection like condoms/dental dams unless you're fluid-bonded with a monogamous partner. Don't trust others with your sexual health.

- Keep condoms, lube, and dams stocked. Being prepared avoids risky situations.

- Get STD tested regularly and ask potential partners their status.

- Never feel pressured into risky behavior. "No" is a complete sentence.

- Be aware of consent – it must be conscious, sober, enthusiastic, and ongoing.

Taking Charge of Your Sexual Health

- Annual STD/STI testing

- OBGYN checkups for reproductive health

- Learn your cycle and body to make informed choices

- Consider contraceptive options that fit your lifestyle

- Research symptoms and don't ignore warning signs

- Prompt treatment for any infections

- Ongoing education as you explore new desires/partners

Knowledge is power. Educate yourself, stand firm on your boundaries, and make smart intimate choices. Take control of your health and embrace sexuality safely. You got this!

9

Everyday Magic

Soul sisters, we've uncovered so much about unleashing our dark goddess energy. But here's the real magic – integrating this fierce feminine power into our regular day-to-day lives.

It's one thing to dance ecstatically under the moon or roar with rage in our bedrooms. But when the lights come up, or the music stops, do we shrink back into our polite persona? Old habits creep in so easily.

True transformation comes from living wholly in our truth every single day. Speaking from the heart no matter who's listening. Owning our space unapologetically. Being radically ourselves without compromise.

This takes practice. Our dark feminine side guides us there when we tune into her voice consistently, not just on full moons or "goddess days." So let's explore...

How do you walk through the world each day? Head down, avoiding eye contact? Or bold strides; head held high? What's your inner dialogue? Fearful and doubting? Or supportive self-talk?

Do you project confidence in displaying your artwork or sharing ideas? Or nervously hope no one notices you? Do you ask directly for raises instead of waiting for offers?

Owning our daily power is a choice. Will we inflate others while deflating ourselves? Or embrace our glorious complexity? The dark goddess in us craves the latter, waiting for us to heed her call consistently.

It's time to infuse magic into the mundane. Bring fierce presence into ordinary moments. Let's shine so brightly the whole damn world takes notice. Our light changes everything when we dare to unleash it fully, no longer dimming our power day to day. We glow from within.

Integrating Practices Into Daily Life

Alright, soul sisters, we've got our dark feminine wisdom unlocked. Now, it's time to integrate that inner magic into our regular routines. Embodying this energy in daily life is where real transformation happens.

Morning Rituals

Start your day centered on your power. Do 10 minutes of meditation or breathwork to ground yourself. Visualize your dark goddess flames igniting within. Say supportive affirmations while looking in the mirror. Set empowering goals for the day.

- Begin with meditation, focusing on deep breathing to center and ground you. Imagine your inner dark goddess flames igniting as you inhale.

- Look in the mirror and recite empowering affirmations like "I am divinely guided" or "My strength overflows."

- Set specific goals aligned with your dark feminine energy – perhaps creative projects to express your wild spirit.

- Create an altar space with crystals, candles, and goddess imagery to anchor your intentions. Sit there journaling or reflecting on the day ahead.

Mindful Minutes

Throughout the day, take mindful minutes to tune into your inner world. Set phone alerts to stop and ask – How am I feeling right now? Am I holding tension anywhere? What do I need in this moment? Check-in with your dark feminine compass.

- Set reminders on your phone/watch to stop throughout the day, take some deep breaths, and check in with yourself.
- Scan your body and release any tension. Unclench your jaws, relax your shoulders down, and soften your gaze.
- Tune into your emotions. Are you repressing any feelings or desires at this moment? Express them creatively.
- Ask your inner wisdom what you need right now. More rest? Different boundaries? Then, act on that intuition.

Creativity & Movement

Make time for unfettered creative expression. Paint, write poetry, sing out loud. Move your body freely, dance sensually, and stretch languorously. These activities channel dark feminine energy.

-       Make time to write, paint, sing, or express yourself through any medium imaginable. Don't censor the messy, dark, feminine creative energy.

-       Dance freely to music, moving your body in ways that feel good. Shake loose any fears or worries. Let your spirit soar.

-       Take sensual bubble baths surrounded by candles, essential oils, and affirmations to pamper and pleasure yourself.

-       Stretch daily with yoga, loosening up energetic blocks and opening your body to its fullest expansion.

Moontime Rituals

Tune into your menstrual cycle's natural rhythm. Mark each moon time with ritual – take rest, reflect, release. Soak in baths, meditate, and share goddess wisdom with other women. Honor this sacred feminine process.

- Mark your moon time by journaling about your menstrual journey, releasing old stagnant energy.

- Create personalized rituals on your period – take a forest bath, craft moon jewelry, and cook nourishing meals. Do what feels rejuvenating.

- Connect with other women by sharing your period experiences. Build community and bond over our cyclic dark feminine mysteries.

Evening Wind Down

Rituals ground us in our purpose and power. When we infuse them throughout our day, our dark feminine light stays vibrant. This magic is always within us, ready to shine!

- Clear your mind by journaling or free-writing to get any swirling thoughts out on paper before bed.

- Write down three things you're grateful for from the day. Recognize the magic and growth moments.

- Take time to pamper yourself – give yourself a facial massage, apply lotions mindfully, and light candles or incense.

- Make your sleep space cozy – clean sheets, soft pajamas, weighted blankets, whatever you need to feel comfortable and calm.

- Spend time reflecting on positive experiences from your day right before bed so you fall asleep with a peaceful mind.

- Listen to relaxing music, meditations, or binaural beats while you drift off to encourage deep rest.

- Keep a dream journal by your bed and record any night visions immediately upon waking. Seek their symbolic wisdom.

- Set a regular bedtime and pre-bed routine so your body prepares for sleep consistently.

Mindfulness, Meditation, Journaling

Here are some simple techniques you can use.

Tune into Your Sense

Mindfulness helps you become more present and aware of your experiences. Try these sensory exercises:

- List 5 things you see. Engage your sense of sight fully. Notice colors, shapes, and textures.

- List 5 things you hear. Tune your ears to subtle ambient sounds around you.

- Hold an object like a rock. Describe its texture and how it feels in your hand. Engage touch.

- Take deep breaths and identify scents in the air. Engage your sense of smell fully.

- Slowly eat something, savoring the flavors. Let the tastes fully come alive.

Observe thoughts and sensations without judgment. Immerse yourself in the present using all five senses. Practicing mindfulness regularly deeply connects you to the moment.

Guided Visualization Meditations

Reprogram your mind with positive new patterns through visualization meditations. Some ideas:

- Picture your dream life in vivid detail – home, career, partner, travel. Make it feel real.

- Visualize yourself confidently achieving a goal – giving a speech, asking for a raise. See yourself succeeding.

- Imagine being filled with qualities you want – courage, joy, freedom. Feel those energies awakening within.

- Picture negative thoughts leaving your mind as swirling smoke. Affirm positive new beliefs replacing them.

Use meditation to shape your inner world. By consistently visualizing dreams realized and ideals embodied, you manifest them in outer reality. Imagination is the first step to creation. Guide your mind intentionally.

Journaling Exercises

Journaling is a powerful way to process emotions, gain self-awareness, and crystallize goals. Here are some ideas:

- Free write your unfiltered thoughts and feelings. Don't hold back.

- List dreams and describe your ideal life in detail. Make it tangible.
- Track patterns around behaviors, relationships, and thought cycles. Increase self-awareness.
- Outline action plans to achieve goals – break them into smaller steps.
- Write encouragement and affirmations to yourself.

However you do journaling, do it regularly without censoring yourself. Putting thoughts on paper is purifying and empowering. You'll gain motivation, clarity, and greater alignment between your inner and outer life.

Seeing the World Through a Lens of Wonder

Let's go over some simple techniques you can use do this;

Adopt Beginner's Mind

Approach your everyday life with childlike curiosity. See the world as if for the first time again. Some ideas:

- Notice details in your environment you normally overlook – textures, colors, sounds. Let the familiar become strange and fascinating again.
- Ask questions nonstop – why is the sky blue? How do plants grow? What makes the bus engine run? Don't let your beginner's mind close.
- Try new routes when commuting. Wander new neighborhoods on weekends. Discover hidden beauty everywhere through an explorer's eyes.

- Have your mind blown by ordinary phenomena – dewdrops, spiderwebs, flower petals, patches of light. Find magic in the mundane.

When you perceive the world with wonder, daily life becomes your classroom. Curiosity leads to presence. Simple joys give deep meaning. Maintain a beginner's mind always.

Cultivate Awe Through Nature

One of the fastest ways to tap into wonder is by spending time in nature. Here's how:

- Take mindful walks through the park or woods. Notice little miracles – the way sunlight filters through trees, the sound of wind through grass. Let nature astonish you.
- Watch a sunrise or sunset. Feel awe at daylight's beginning and ending. Marvel at colors painting the vast sky. Witness nature's artistry.

- Stargaze at night. Feel existential wonder at the infinity above you. Your problems shrink in perspective.

- Plant seeds and watch them grow. Be amazed as tiny sprouts transform into huge blooming plants. Participate in this natural wonder.

When you connect with nature, childlike awe comes alive. Hardened perspectives soften. You tap into the current of magic that animates the mundane world. Daily life glows with newfound fascination.

Finding Beauty and Joy in the Present

Nothing ignites the fire in us, sis, like enjoying the beauty of the present.

Savor Ordinary Moments

Life is made up of tiny experiences. Don't just rush through them – savor the details! Here's how:

- Eat slowly without distractions. Appreciate flavors and textures. Make meals mindful rituals.

- Inhale the aroma of morning coffee deeply before drinking. Let the smell envelop you.

- Listen to music with eyes closed, visualizing the melodies and rhythms. Be engulfed.

- Feel the warmth of the sun or breeze on your skin. Tune into subtle sensations.

- Engage all your senses during walks. Notice vivid colors, chirping birds, and crunchy leaves underfoot.

When you immerse yourself in ordinary moments, extraordinary beauty reveals itself. Life becomes technicolor. Even mundane moments shimmer with subtle miracles when experienced fully.

Find Joy in Small Pleasures

Train your mind to find delight in simple things:

- Cozy up with a blanket on the couch with tea – savor the warmth and comfort. Feel immersed in coziness.

- Doodle patterns mindfully, enjoying the feeling of pen gliding over paper. Lose yourself in the flow state.

- Take bubble baths surrounded by candles, music, and wine. Turn bathing into a sensual ritual.

- Cook or bake something you love. Appreciate the textures, scents, and flavors. Feel pride in nourishing yourself.

- Cuddle a pet. Stroke its soft fur mindfully. Soak in the affection.

Strings of mini joys make up your days. The more you open your mind and senses to life's simple pleasures, the more contentment and lightness you will feel. Delight in small beauties always.

10

Sisterhood and Service

Sis, remember that empowerment is not just about you. It's about uplifting your communities, too. You have so much wisdom to offer now – share it!

Support other women on their journeys. Volunteer, mentor, collaborate. Help local women's organizations. Or maybe start your own meetup or workshop series!

Your sisters need you. I know you can get lost in your growth sometimes. But true power means being of service. Show up for girls who need guidance. Use your experiences to light their path. Remind them of their inner magic.

And teach the men in your life how to honor the queens around them. Show them empowerment is not a competition - we can uplift each other. Evolve toxic mindsets through compassion.

Living your purpose often means helping others live theirs. Rise by lifting others. Build networks of possibility, healing, and support. Share your hard-won knowledge. Keep paying forward the gifts you've received.

The collective is empowered one woman at a time. Womanhood is your heritage – honor it through service. However you choose to contribute, know that you have so much brightness to offer this world. Shine on, Queen!

The Power of Female Friendships

Sis, surrounding yourself with empowered queens is key for continuing growth. Here's how female friendships boost confidence:

- Advice from women who've been there offers instant clarity when you're unsure of your next steps. Their realness keeps you accountable.

- Seeing your friends shine reminds you of your inner magic. Their wins feel like yours, too.

- Laughing together lightens any struggle. Stress and tears turn to belly laughs in a girlfriend's presence.

- Late-night conversations crack open your world. You see possibilities beyond limitations.

- Dance parties with the girls get your sexy swag going. You remember your goddess energy.

- Group workouts motivate you to push harder and be your best self. Competition is healthy.

Make sisterhood a priority. Plan regular quality time together – not just quick coffee dates or texts. Get vulnerable about dreams, fears, and insecurities. Your circle of trust becomes your safety net.

When you have real friends who accept every part of you, judgment disappears. This gives you the freedom to continue growing and rising. Surround yourself with queens who want the same.

Serving Others Through Volunteering

Once you've done personal growth work, it feels amazing to pay it forward. Volunteer with organizations that empower women and girls. Here are some meaningful ways to contribute:

- Mentor teen girls through groups like Girls Inc. Share your experiences. Guide them in building confidence, setting goals, and embracing womanhood.

- Teach classes on skills you have – fitness, art, writing, music, etc. Local women's centers often need teachers. Inspire others with your talents.

- Organize donation drives for women's shelters – clothes, toiletries, school supplies for kids. Help women gain stability during hard times.

- Offer free classes on women's health/wellness – nutrition, stress management, and self-care. These resources uplift.

- Use social media to spotlight women-owned businesses and causes. Amplify important work.

- Fundraise or donate to women's organizations. Look for grassroots groups making a direct local impact.

However you volunteer, commit to doing it consistently. When you show up reliably, you demonstrate true dedication and service. This builds trust and allows you to see tangible progress.

Helping others also helps you. Using your gifts gives deep purpose. You gain perspective on your resilience by observing women overcoming challenges. And sisterhood grew stronger. Keep showing up, Queen.

Uplifting Other Women

A rising tide lifts all ships, sis. As you grow into your power, bring other women along:

- Give sincere compliments. Praise her style, talents, and character. Watch her light up.

- Listen deeply. Be a non-judging ear for her to confide in. Feeling heard builds trust.

- Recommend books/podcasts you love that uplifted you. Share tools that helped your journey.

- Introduce her to contacts who could help her career/dreams. Use your connections to open doors.

- Validate her feelings. If she shares struggles, say, "You're not alone in this." Remind her of inner strength.

- Spot leadership potential. Encourage her to take on new responsibilities/challenges. Believe in her.

- Offer feedback to help her grow. Be constructively honest. Guide gently, not critically.

- Collaborate on projects. Brainstorming together breeds creativity.

- Celebrate her wins as if they're yours! Hype her up. Toast achievements.

There's too much woman-on-woman envy and gossip already. We rise together by lifting each other. Share your light. Give what you need most when growing into your power. All women deserve to feel seen.

Leaving a Legacy of Love

When your time on earth ends, how do you want to be remembered, Queen? Live your life, leaving a legacy of love.

- Put kindness first. All the achievements in the world mean nothing without caring for others.

- Forgive freely. Holding grudges poisons your soul. Release them.

- Mentor those who are lost. Use your hard-won wisdom to guide and reassure.

- Create beauty. Share your gifts, talents, and art with the world.

- Spread joy. Tell jokes, give hugs, and bring communities together in celebration.

- Stand up for truth and justice. Even when it's unpopular. Do what's right over what's easy.

- -

- Honor Mother Earth. Live sustainably. Protect nature and its gifts for future generations.

- Help those in need. Donate, volunteer, and reach out a hand. Alleviate suffering wherever you can.

- Listen more than you speak. Remaining open and curious keeps your heart expanding.

- Express gratitude. For big and small blessings. Feeling and showing appreciation ascends you higher.

- Follow your purpose. Use your unique talents to leave the world better than you found it.

Who you are and how you live matters. Create a wave of light with your every action. Uplift others each day. Your essence echoes through time. Craft a legacy defined by compassion and wisdom.

Conclusion

I n the grand finale of our dark feminine journey — unleash your empowered self!

We've been through it all together, my Queen. We tended to your dark side and shadows. You discovered new confidence through bold body language. Your truest feelings flowed onto journal pages.

Now, here we are at the finish line, where it all comes together. You've done the inner work and are prepared for an empowered new chapter. The old, limited you have been shed. A wiser, braver goddess rises in her place.

It's time to take this newfound sense of mission out into the world. Speak your truth boldly. Keep growing your self-love and shooting down fears. And trust that you have everything you need within. I can't wait to see the change you create!

Now, head into your bright future with confidence. And when challenges arise, remember: the dark feminine mystique has your back. Wield it proudly, unapologetically, fiercely. Stay wild at heart, and keep your eyes on the horizon. Your life is just beginning, superstar!

Cheers to Your Journey

Take a moment to celebrate how far you've come, Queen! Pour a drink, put on music, and give a toast to yourself. Speak out loud about all you've learned and accomplished. Soak in this victory. You uncovered your dark side, practiced bold body language, and boosted your confidence tremendously. Reflect on the growth you've made – write it down to read when you need motivation.

And keep the momentum going. Make a list of books, podcasts, and other resources to continue expanding your inner goddess. Share recommendations with girlfriends to stay inspired together. Growth is lifelong. Now, go shake things up armed with your empowered, dark, feminine energy!

Continued Femme Exploration

This is just the start of your empowerment journey, Queen. To keep growing, join a community of badass women – an online group, local meetup, and networking circle. Having a sisterhood cheers you on as you continue rising into your power.

And never stop exploring new parts of your dark feminine energy. Make it a lifelong practice to push boundaries, ask bold questions, and redefine womanhood on your terms. You have an eternity of untapped potential within.

So, soak up new mentors and resources constantly. Immerse yourself in empowering spaces that inspire you to show up bravely. Keep evolving into your fullest expression.

The world needs your light and conviction more than ever. Now, take your new wisdom and confidence out there – speak the truth, uplift others, and shatter glass ceilings. I can't wait to see the change you create. This is just the beginning!

GET YOUR BONUSES HERE!

BONUS 1: The 90-Day Dark Feminine Energy Prompts

BONUS 2: Activation Prompt Guide

SCAN HERE
for the Activation Prompts Guide

www.ingramcontent.com/pod-product-compliance
Lightning Source LLC
Chambersburg PA
CBHW050732260726
48661CB00001B/195